Every four years, the greatest footballers on Earth compete for their countries in the FIFA World Cup.

In 2026, 48 men's teams will compete in Canada, Mexico and the United States to lift the trophy.

Then the following year in Brazil, 32 teams will play in the Women's World Cup.

This book is all about the players who have performed brilliantly at the World Cup.

Messi started playing football as soon as he could walk. He joined the Spanish football club Barcelona when he was 13 years old. He played for Paris St Germain in France and then Inter Miami in the United States.

Messi is one of the fastest players ever – reaching speeds of more than 32 kilometres per hour. Nobody dribbles the ball at speed like Messi!

He is also incredible at tricks like nutmegs, where a player moves the ball between his opponent's legs.

Messi led Argentina to victory at the World Cup in 2022. He scored twice in the final against France. Can Messi and Argentina win it again?

This is Mbappe's favourite goal celebration.
He slides along the ground on his knees and folds his
arms. You will probably see this in the World Cup...
because Mbappe scores lots and lots of goals.

When Mbappe was only 19 years old, he played for France in the 2018 World Cup final. He scored and France won the trophy!

Just four years later, he faced his childhood hero Lionel Messi in the 2022 World Cup final.

France lost to Argentina, but Mbappe scored an amazing hat-trick. (That's three goals in a game.)

Sam has played in four World Cups already!
In 2019, she became the only Australian ever to score
a hat-trick in the tournament.

The world will be watching Sam's
moves at the next Women's World Cup.

HARRY KANE is the captain of England.

The ultimate striker, he is incredible at scoring goals, and he is already a football legend.

As a boy, Kane wanted to play for his local team, the Premier League side Tottenham Hotspur... and his dream came true. Harry signed for them when he was just 11.

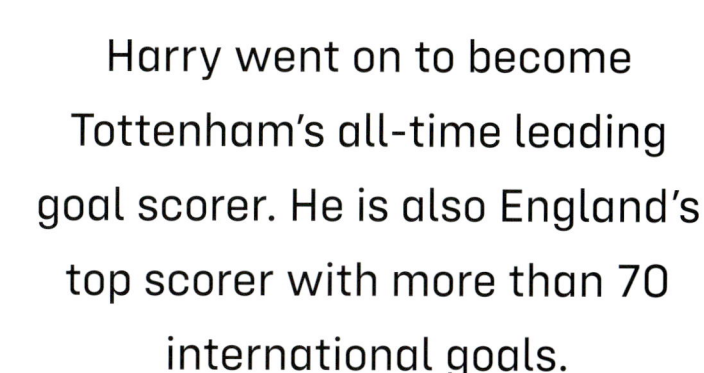

Harry went on to become Tottenham's all-time leading goal scorer. He is also England's top scorer with more than 70 international goals.

England played in the semi-final of the World Cup in 2018. They didn't win, but Kane scored six goals in the tournament, winning him the World Cup Golden Boot. (That's the award for the top goalscorer.)

Kane won another Golden Boot at Euro 2024 – a tournament between the top countries in Europe. He led his team all the way to the final.

With Kane as England's captain, anything is possible!

At the Olympic Games in Paris in 2024, she scored three goals that helped the United States to win gold.

Together with her United States teammates Trinity Rodman and Mallory Swanson, Wilson is part of an unstoppable goalscoring trio.

Hey, **NEYMAR!**

This awesome Brazilian striker's full name is Neymar da Silva Santos Júnior, but most people know him as Neymar.

Neymar grew up playing a type of football called futsal.

It is played on a small, hard court, with a little ball.

Futsal players move skilfully and learn cool tricks.

Neymar is one of the most entertaining strikers in football. He takes amazing shots at goal, and no one does the rainbow flick quite like him!

He helped the Brazil football team to win an Olympic gold medal, and he has played for Brazil in three World Cups.

Neymar became Brazil's top scorer ever after he broke the record set by the Brazilian legend Pelé. Neymar is back after an injury and could play at the next World Cup!

He is brilliant at just about everything – dribbling, making space, tricks, penalties, free-kicks... and most importantly, he scores heaps of goals.

Ronaldo has played for his country more than any other player in the world, and he has scored the most international goals ever.

This football superstar is **SON HEUNG-MIN,** captain of South Korea.

He is one of the finest attacking players in the game. Son is fast, with super ball control, and he always hits the back of the net.

Son has scored goals in three World Cups since 2014 – and he's never been more ready for the next one in 2026!

These players could be the

FUTURE STARS

of the world cup!

JUDE BELLINGHAM

This amazing all-rounder has played for England since he was 17. He also stars for one of the world's top clubs, Real Madrid.

LAMINE YAMAL

When he was just 16, Yamal became the youngest person ever to play for AND score for Spain. Just one year later, he helped Spain to win Euro 2024.

YANG MIN-HYEOK

This speedy winger played for South Korea in the Under-17 Asian Cup and World Cup. Now is his chance to shine for South Korea's senior side.

TRINITY RODMAN

Rodman was a star forward for the United States women's team when they won a gold medal at the 2024 Olympic Games.

There are magic moments at every World Cup, where players show their skills and score amazing goals, and make their fans incredibly happy.

WHO WILL BECOME YOUR WORLD CUP HERO?